Your Vision Board Must Only Have Positive Statements.

By the end of reading this you will know why I included your template,

contact me if you have any questions.

Your Name _____

Mission Statement _____

Moving Towards Values & Rules
1
2
3
4
5
6
7
8
9
10
11
12

Moving Away From Values & Rules
1
2
3
4
5
6
7
8
9
10
11
12

My New Primary Question _____

My Power Virtues
1
2
3

My Top Three One Year Goals
1
2
3

My Ultimate Vision
_____
_____
_____

Lisa Christiansen Companies ©

1

~∞~

The Biggest Compliment you can give me is to refer this to a friend and Pay it forward.

In the beginning man has been lead away from his destiny without ever knowing why. Man has been lead unwillingly just as sheep away from his true destiny. Understanding how and why YOU yourself have been lead away from YOUR true DESTINY will not only engage you into discovery of your destiny but then in the aid of others.

About the Author

For the past two decades, **Lisa Christiansen** has served as advisor to heads of state, peak performers in sports, business, politics and entertainment, as well as leaders around the globe. Lisa Christiansen is the global authority on Leadership Psychology; a recognized authority on the psychology of leadership and human behavior, with a Doctorate in Exercise and Nutritional Sciences and a degree in psychology.

Dr. Lisa Christiansen has helped millions of people create extraordinary lives globally. Her expertise and guidance has enriched the lives of icons such as pop superstar Kelly Clarkson, Olympian Dara Torres, and super star Patrick Dempsey. Visit her website for more information http://www.drlisacoaching.com

I dedicate this book to God first as I dedicate this book to all of you; God gave a gift to the world when you were born; a person who loves and cares, who sees a person's need and fills it, who encourages and lifts people up, who spends energy on others rather than himself, who touches each life he enters & makes a difference in the world. May the love you have shown to others return to you multiplied.

DISCLAIMER:

The Gold does not chase the prospector so don't just stand around waiting for it to show up.

> The characteristic of genuine heroism is its persistency. All men have wandering impulses, fits and starts of generosity. But when you have resolved to be great, abide by yourself, and do not try to reconcile yourself with the world. The heroic cannot be common, or the common heroic.
>
> **~Ralph Waldo Emerson**

First we make our choices then our choices make us... What decision will you make today to create the tomorrow you are committed to???

1) What am I doing today to get what I want?

2) Will this behavior improve my situation and move me towards what I want?... or am I settling?

3) How would the person I want to be do the thing I am about to do?

4) Who do I have to become to attract the success I want?

5) Am I willing to accept the consequences of not changing.

6) Who is in control?

7) Am I practicing to improve or doing just enough to get by?

8) What don't I SEE?

9) If my Board of Directors could see my level of effort, focus and intensity, would I get a raise or get fired?

10) Am I willing to do whatever it takes?

Pen and Highlighter? Maybe Not...

I'd welcome you to have a pen and a highlighter at the ready while you are reading this book, also, you may want to have a pen and notebook ready in case you feel the urge to make a note or two, well this may be where a highlighter may be useful.

This little book is filled with some interesting information that you may or may not find useful and interesting. You may find some of the skills and techniques useful in your network marketing business, as well as your regular 9 to 5 job if you have one of those. And you may also find it useful in your interpersonal relationships as well.

However you may not find it so helpful with your self-dialoging, or conversations you may or may not have with you. Although on the other hand you may find it useful when using it for a reference for your motivational self-talk.

Some of the concepts in this book, might work, may work sometimes, or might not ever work at all; however you can rest assured absolutely NONE of the ideas in this book will work if you never try them, and NONE of these ideas will ever grow legs and walk off the page leaving the page blank in their absence.

Introduction

This book is about the art of communication, more importantly about human communication.

Words are powerful; it is not what you say it is what the listener hears.
It is about saying what you mean, meaning what you say, and saying it with meaning, in a way that is congruent with your intention. What is most important is to learn to understand the art of communication and to cultivate it in such a way that it will most captivate the attention of the greatest number of people. You must ask how, what, when, where, and why; what will move people? You want to tell it like it is in a way that it will get the attention of the most people. We will also discuss guided decisions utilizing the simple process of directed choice, this will be discussed here also, although slightly later as you read more.

Communicating on purpose, with a purpose, and purposely doing so with the intent of getting a point, a thought, or an idea across to your listener.

I have written this book to be playful, silly, while educational. So let's have some fun! Sit back, relax, and enjoy the first day of the rest of your life as you learn to communicate in a way that will redefine your future and design your life. You already know how to survive now it's time to live...

Just two people relaxing having somewhat of a one sided conversation, since I will be doing most of the talking, unless of course you feel the need to chime in with a comment or two.

Just think of it as a casual conversation about communication, and about communicating on a different level, with the intention of communicating first and foremost in mind.

Communicating, talking, moving, acting, miming, singing, humming, are all types of communicating. Any time you are conveying a message to others you are actively engaged in communication, and as long as you are communicating it is always a good idea to do it on purpose.

Accidental communication could be embarrassing, and it is known to be the leading cause of miscommunication, and although curiosity is what might have killed the cat, miscommunication is what lead the cat to the room full of rocking chairs, just like the saying goes. "More nervous than a long tailed cat in a room full of rocking chairs."

You may have guessed by now this book will be slightly humorous, and or just plain corny, depending on how you chose to see it. But make no mistake this book is just that, a book, and there may just be one or two things you might like to read within the confines of the pages therein.

I am going to ask you a question and I want you to be honest, are you willing to play full out and be fun, playful, curious and willing to learn for our short time together while you are reading this book?

Good glad to hear it, because I already agreed to as well, so let's have some fun learn a thing or two and enjoy this time together, shall we?

If this is the first book of mine that you have read then you should be catching on by now I enjoy having fun and I enjoy coaching. You are probably wondering right about now if this book is going to get even a little serious, am I right?

Well it already has, in coaching it is important to get the listeners attention, in this case your attention and the quickest, easiest and most fun way to do that is with humor. If you have been paying attention thus far, and your unconscious mind is open and receptive, you are beginning to earn already without you even knowing it.

As you read on I will be referencing back to various things I have already written thus far, and you will undoubtedly go back and re-read it and have an aha moment. That is good, that simply means the light bulb is going on for you and your mind is awake, because of course everyone knows it's hard for the mind to sleep when the light bulb is on.

Rituals, Trust & Intention . . .

"Talk all you want to, Flores says, but if you want to act powerfully, you need to master "speech acts": language rituals that build trust between colleagues and customers, word practices that open your eyes to new possibilities. Speech acts are powerful because most of the actions that people engage in -- in business, in marriage, in parenting -- are carried out through conversation. But most people speak without intention; they simply say whatever comes to mind. Speak with intention, and your actions take on new purpose. Speak with power, and you act with power." (quote from article excerpt written by Harriet Rubin - The Power of Words Fast Company.com

"Speech acts," interesting combination of words, wouldn't you agree?

Speaking without intention? How could this be? Someone talks to you and you answer right, how hard could that be? "hi, how are you?" you simply answer, "doing well." oops, is that proper English? Shouldn't it be, "doing well?" or maybe, "hi, how are you," is too formal for your day to day interactions, maybe it sounds more like, "yo, sup?" and then you answer, "nada dawg, u?"

Depending on your situation both are appropriate greetings and replies, the second one probably has more meaning and heartfelt emotions than the first one. It is a language almost all its own, with nuances and slight variations that induces a sense of connection on a deeper level.

"Slang" of the old days has evolved and morphed into almost a language of its own; however the communication is deeper than you might expect. It is almost a coded language and if you don't know the code you are not readily accepted, and if you try to fake it, it will be noticed immediately.

Speech acts are powerful because we all do it, everyday, everywhere, all the time. Do you speak without intention, and simply say whatever comes to mind?

The rituals of communication are important part of communication and you should pay attention to be aware of them.

Rituals like, tone of voice, actual words used, how the words are used, rate of speech, and not to mention your body language. At any given time all of these elements are used to convey your message. You are actually communicating with your whole body, from your eyes to your toes.

Saying what you mean is not just about the words, it's about the whole message.

Words

What words are you using?

You walk up to a prospect in your Networking Business, and what do you say? Does it command respect, does it have a certain charm, does it lack sincerity, and does it portray someone who is successful or someone at the edge of their rope?

Again the words you say are not the whole message. What if I were to walk up to you and introduce myself, "Hello, My name is Lisa." nothing wrong in that right? What if I just had an argument with a
customer service rep. from my cell phone company about calls to Argentina that I never made and they say I owe $9,000.00 and I better whip out my credit card to pay for these charges or they will shut off my phone, and then I come over to you and say, "HELLO, MY NAME IS LISA!" Do you think there will be a different response on your part?

I know that is an extreme example, but it does make my point. Here you are in network marketing and maybe your spouse or relatives are constantly hounding you about being in this business, they do not understand, they ridicule you, condemn you, bash your business ideas, and they chastise you in public about it every chance they get. Then you come to the meeting, you invited 35 people to join you and only 3 showed up, and the one who said they would sign up tonight after the meeting didn't even show up, and then you walk over to say hi to me. Do you think there is going to be just a little bit of a mixed message in there somewhere?

Your language and the way you stand and speak is going to give me the message that you are desperate, if you are desperate and you have been doing this business for a couple years now and still struggling, what kind of message is that going to send to your prospects?

I know there are many techniques and ways around this, and this book is not about those, this is about communication, about your intention of your communication, and speaking with intention. I will leave the other techniques for another day.

"Speak with power and you act with power." Speak without power, and you act as if you have no power. Are you powerful in your communication, or are your weak?

Do people enjoy listening to you?

Confusion says, "?"

Take a look at the title of this book once again. What does it say?

Now look at the picture on the cover, what does that say?

Are the words and the picture saying the same thing?

Oh, oh, I know some of you reading this now are saying, what a minute the words and the pictures are giving the same message, but the colors of the words are not giving the right message.

WOW! Eureka, you've found it! The colors are not giving off the same message, does that change the meaning of the title? It might not change the meaning, but it does change the mood when reading it. It actually sends mixed messages to the brain about the message and that incongruent message is enough to make you pause for a brief moment.

Now read the title, by the colors, in other words, instead of Green sheep, it would be White sheep, and so on, then come right back. I'll wait.......

Well how did it go? Not so easy huh? Just that little difference makes a world of difference in how you read the words.

Red   Blue   Green

Orange   Yellow   Purple

Read the words out loud, easy enough right? Now, read the words but say the colors. Not quite so easy was it?

Imagine what it would be like if all your conversations with your clients, down line, up line, prospects, spouse, children and friends were like this. Your words are not congruent with your colors, or messages, how frustrating would that be?

If your listener is confused about the message you are conveying, you both lose.

U.T.S.

No, it's not a new disease, U.T.S. simply means Undeniably Truthful Statements. These are statements your listener cannot argue with, because they are undeniably truthful.

Take a look at the cover again, what do the words say? And what does the picture show? It's the same thing, so it is undeniably truthful. You cannot argue the point. This is the best way to avoid arguments and disagreements, and people finding fault with what you say.

Before we go another second together, I hear a few of you reading this book and murmuring to yourself in disagreement about the cover. You say, "the sheep is not all brown, the grass is not totally green, it's more of an olive green, and the sky is not totally blue, there are clouds in the sky.

The people thinking that now, you are known as a (mismatcher); as a mismatcher you almost instantly notice the differences in everything, and can be very quick to point it out to others.

We are all like that to a certain degree, and in certain situations, however mismatchers take it one step further. It can be annoying, and bother some, however when communicating with people it is important to know how to communicate with mismatchers as well. We will get into that in a moment or two.

For now let's focus our thoughts on U.T.S. When you communicate it is a good idea not to rub people the wrong way. For instance you walk up to someone you've been wanting to meet for a long time, you are worried about making a good impression and you finally get up the nerve to walk up to them and introduce yourself at a friends get-together and it goes all wrong.

"Hi, my name is Lisa; it's such a pleasure to meet you. I did not know you were pregnant, how far along are you, when is the baby due?" And she answers, "I'm not pregnant." OOPS!!!!

How could I have avoided that one?

By noticing undeniably truthful things about her, her hair, her dress, her makeup, her accomplishments, the event we are at, there are many things I could have said that would not have been WRONG!

Do you ever do that with your prospects? You have a meeting with them and you ask a harmless question like, have you ever thought of redecorating your home; I have someone in my organization who could do wonders with your place. And they respond, we just redecorated last month. OOPS!

Maybe that is a little extreme for an example? How about this, the prospect meets you at a local café, and you want to get them something to drink, you ask if they would like a cup of coffee and they say, "I don't drink coffee," to which you respond, "really, you look like a coffee drinker." OOPS again!

What should you have done? Pick out something that is undeniably truthful. There are also undeniably truthful events, you could make a comment about one of those.

For example:

The scent of the coffee in the air, the muffins, all the people relaxing, it is a comfortable atmosphere, I think I will join in. What would you like a drink as well?

There's not much to argue with about that little interaction. Just stating undeniably truthful events, and leading with a simple imbedded suggestion, and since you are in a café it only stands to reason that your guest might want something to drink also.

Here you are walking in your local electronics store, and a

salesman approaches you, and asks, "Is there anything in particular I can help you find?"

Makes me want to pull my hair out by the roots. Help me find what I am looking for, are you serious, it's not like things are hidden away somewhere. I can find it on my own, you want to be of service get out of the way, you're standing on my foot.

It's not always that bad, but more times than not it is. The salesman would get a lot further with UTS, and by not standing on my foot, that is always a big plus with me.

What he should have done was casually take notice of what I was doing, where I was looking and then approach me saying something like; "welcome to (store name) a place I like to call 'home' 9 hours a day, and like my home I know where almost everything is, unless it was moved in the middle of the night. I noticed you were looking at (whatever I was looking at) as you can see there are a few of them right here in front of you and you will notice a few more as you walk along, they're hiding on a shelf (in aisle 5) should you find yourself wondering if you can get a demo, I'll be here in the area keeping an eye on things just let me know and I'll be right there."

That is how it should be done, or something close to that.

Doing it Right for a Change

I was shopping one day in a local big chain electronics store, when I was approached by such a sales professional. Impressed with his abilities, I proceeded to shop, and asked him questions about sales, to which surprisingly enough he knew the right answers.

While at the register checking out, with my big screen T.V. surround sound system, my first HP iPaq palm computer/cell phone, and the one item I came in for, a Wi-Fi wireless router for my computers.

I asked the sales professional if he has heard of Dr. Donald Moine, he said he has and that he has his book, Unlimited Selling Power.   Impressed with his knowledge of sales and how he expertly handled my shopping experience, and me I had to ask where did he learn how to do this.

He told me, he finally got his chance to break out of the stockroom and enter the world of sales, moving to the sales floor was his dream come true, but 3 months later that dream was about to be crashed against the rocks of despair. He was failing as a sales person, his sales were so low management issued him a final written warning, if he did not bring his sales up in 30 days he would be fired.

He heard of a sales training being held at the Marriott just down the street, and decided to put the ticket on his credit card and attend.

The seminar he attended was almost a year ago, now I was really curious. I was shocked to learn that this sales professional attended a seminar almost a year ago and is still practicing the skills and techniques he had learned.

I had to ask, since I was at that very hotel almost a year ago, "who's seminar was it that you attended?" He said of course Lisa, it was yours. He proceeded to tell me, he has gone on to break almost every sales record to date, and has been promoted twice and is now the Sales Floor Manager.

He went on to tell me the exact moment he decided to take the action needed to learn all he could about sales. It was when I had a man and a woman who did not know each other come up to the stage and tell me the one thing they could find in a store and would never buy.

And then he watched intently as I demonstrated for the audience how to sell them as a couple to buy those very things, without using high pressure, without tricking them, and have them actually convince me why they needed to buy it now.

That was the turning point for him. I was simply amazed at his applying these skills so diligently and so thoroughly.

Undeniably truthful statements are a very powerful form of communication.

One author who shall remain nameless, became one of the most widely known authors in the world, has sold more books on his chosen topic than any other person in history. It wasn't until several years later, and several millions of dollars in profits and a few successful follow up books did people begin to understand his books were not all they were hyped-up to be, and his credentials were questionable at best.

Did his books help some people? I am sure on some level someone somewhere was able to receive at least a little help. His seminars were sold out, his books sold off the shelves, he was on talk shows, and it was not till several years later that people were starting to see the forest despite the trees. I know you are eager to learn who this man is, and I cannot tell you, because his attorney aggressively
pursues anyone who attempts to state the facts around this man's rise to success. Then I'll get a cease and desist order and threats of lawsuit and then I will have to rewrite this little book.

So why bother....

Nonetheless his best sellers were based on little more than undeniably Truthful Statements.

People would read the books, think in the back of their minds, "that is so much like me, she is so dead on, there is no way anything else in the book can be inaccurate." And that is precisely why the books were written the way they were, how can you dispute a book based on undeniably truthful statements? You can't, at every turn there is a logical and easy to explain answer to your question.

You can use undeniably truthful statements to build your business and relationships that will grow and mature into lifelong friendships, without having to resort to the tactics of that author.

Your mission, should you decide to accept it, is to study, do, and teach these techniques and watch your organization grow.

Building Your Business with U.T.S.

Undeniably truthful statements start with easily observable events, or actions. These are things that you can easily see and observe.

Everything and anything around you is observable, and noticeable.

You can also use the business opportunity; there is a common thread between you and your prospects. You are interested in the:

Freedom   **Income potential**   **Lifestyle**

Friendships   **Travel**   **Residuals**

This is a business that can truly allow you to have it all, if you have what it takes to go for your dreams. Building your business using UTS, an interesting thought.

Many times in this business you hear so much talk about overcoming objections, and then someone else says, there are never any real objections, just questions, then someone goes on to tell you that the prospect is not objecting to you, or rejecting you, it's just the timing.

So what do you believe?

Believe it all if you want to, remember what is true for you, is indeed true for you. That does not mean it is gospel truth, it just means it is true for you, nothing more than that, and from time to time you will allow certain events to shape and twist and turn some of those truths to mean something new and improved.

Looking at building your business with UTS, is just another way of looking at communicating with your prospect.

For example, you know your prospect is a little nervous about network marketing, what do you do? Most representatives I have come across over the years try to overcompensate for their prospects apprehension and cold feet.

They overcompensate by anticipating the objections, and answer them before they come up. This is a good approach but not the ideal approach. Old school salesmen will tell you to flat out ignore the initial apprehension and objections, if they are real they will come up again. Once again not the ideal way to approach this situation.

Handling this situation with UTS, takes a slightly new approach, first as you might have already guessed, simply state the undeniably truthful event. "I can see you are a little apprehensive."

What are they going to say, "No I'm not, your eyes are wrong, you're seeing things?" They will be slightly more relaxed because you noticed it and they no longer need to hide it from you because they know you see the apprehension and you are not freaking out, so it is safe for them to feel this way now.

Here is where old school salesmen try to sell the prospect on all the reasons why they should overcome their fears. NOT YOU though. Selling at this point is not your job, only stating the obvious that is all you are supposed to be doing at this point.

Others will pull out the old, feel, felt, found technique. This is not necessary, it could be used here but not necessary at this point.

Reading Minds???

I am going to share with you a very closely guarded secret; this is where you use the ultimate undeniably truthful statement, the Forced Mind Read. (combined with embedded commands)

Before you jump out of your seat screaming and running for the door, I have to explain, you are not really reading anyone's mind here. It is a technique used to build more rapport and let your prospect become more relaxed. (I will not cover embedded commands in this book that will be another time.)

You can see they are apprehensive, you state as such and then simply say, "you're probably wondering what your family will say when they ask you about your new business and you tell them it is network marketing, right? (This is an example; you have to use your prospects state of mind and what you know of them to make this type of statement. Without knowing it can you spot the embedded commands? This will give you a head start on my other book…)

I can't just look at my prospect and say, " you're probably thinking about the last time you went to the zoo and you stopped by the monkey exhibit and watched as the monkeys played and started throwing poop at each other." That might be a true event for them, however that is NOT what they are thinking about at this precise moment, at least not before now that is.

There is a SECRET within the confines of this page can you tell me what it is? The secret has to do with the Ultimate Undeniably Truthful Statement.

Did you find it?

That secret is important for you to remember. If you have children this should be easy for you to understand.

Imagine you are at the breakfast table, and the children are at the table reaching for glasses of juice, and boxes of cereal, and toys and whatever else they can manage to grab or touch. Then you notice the chaos, and tell them to be careful not to spill the milk. Not more than 15 seconds later, there goes the milk.

Let me ask you, why not spill the juice? The juice would have been easier to spill; it is in the glass, the milk is in the carton. There are three ways to spill the milk,
1. To tip over an open container
2. The top pops off when it tips or falls off the table.
3. To spill it while pouring it, the milk shifts, their tiny muscles cannot handle the shifting weight fast enough and viola milk fills the bowl instantly, and on to the table and then the floor.

So why the milk?

That's the secret found on the page before this one. Go back now and see if you can find it.

Did you find it now?

Here is the answer, **they were not thinking of spilling anything, until you put the idea into their mind**. Forced Mind Read, and embedded command.

It is not a mind read at all, as the name would suggest, it is actually you putting the thought in the listeners mind.

There is a famous sales trainer out there in the world today, that actually talks about how to do a variation of this skill, however he does it in a way that forces the prospect to correct his statement.

For example he would say, "If I understand you correctly, you are looking for a car in Yellow." The prospect would then correct him, by stating, "Not yellow, bright orange," or whatever color they want. The salesman forced the prospect to correct him, by making an erroneous statement.

This forced mind read is not like that. You are actually directing to a certain degree the thoughts of your prospect without tricking them in anyway. This is not a trick, it is a skill. It is a way of speaking with intention. Speech Acts as mentioned on page 9.

Tricky Skills of Magic

Like a magician I can tell what card you will pick…

PLAY ALONG

What if I told you that I could predict 100% of the time which card you will pick out of a deck of playing cards, just by asking a few questions. Would you believe me?

Imagine now, I am holding a deck of cards, which do you prefer red or black suits?

And of the red and black if I put the red aside that leaves the black doesn't it?

Of the Black suits which do you prefer clubs or spades? If I put the clubs aside, that leaves the spades right?

With the spade as within any of the suits of cards there are face cards and there are numbered cards, which would you prefer the face cards or the numbered cards?

If I put the numbered cards aside that would leave the face cards wouldn't it?

Of the face cards there is the Ace, King, Queen, and Jack, of these cards which do you prefer? The Ace and King or the Queen and Jack?

If I take the Queen and Jack and place them aside with the rest of the deck, that would leave the Ace and King right? Of the Ace and King which do you prefer?

If I place the King with the rest of the deck that would leave the Ace of Spades wouldn't it?

Turn the page.

Ready for the Million Dollar SECRET?

I know that is a simple trick, however the skills used in that trick are real. **Mostly UTS, nothing more**.

I know in the back of your mind you are wondering if I was really able to have two people who don't know each other come up on stage and buy a product they normally would never buy. The answer is yes.

However let's take a look at how you can make that happen.

Think about a product you might find in a normal store that you would almost never buy.

For most men they would NEVER buy feminine hygiene products, and for women this is a little more difficult, because women love to shop. They shop for themselves and friends, neighbors, family, so they really love to buy almost anything. So you can imagine how hard it was on stage to get the woman to think of something she would not like to buy. She decided on a fishing pole, she would not ever picture herself buying a fishing pole.

So now you have an idea of what the challenge was like.

The first thing is to link the two together emotionally, kind of like making friends on the spot. I did this by noticing similarities between them, and linking them together with UTS.

Then simply using what you have learned in this little book, began to ask questions based on observable facts, made some simple conclusions, waited for a response, and asked some more.

Asking both of them simultaneously and at times independently of each other. Gaining opposing and differing opinions from time to time. Reminding you to use almost exclusively UTS, coupled with forced mind reads.

And viola he agreed, the next time his wife needed he would volunteer to help out and go to the store with a list and make the purchase for her, his way of saying, "I love you." And she remembered an uncle who loves to fish whom she had not seen in many years, and remembered spending time with him while he would be fishing, when she was a little girl and how she loved that time with her uncle, and decided a custom $1,500.00 fishing pole would be the perfect gift for him.

Whereas before, out of all the things she said she would not ever buy, this is the one item she said she would never have a reason in a million years to buy and doesn't endorse fishing, this is the one item she was convinced you could not get her to buy. Reassuring her you aren't there to make her do anything.

More important than just the words you use and the UTS, your tone of voice, at times taking on the role of wife, and then uncle, and then the couple on stage with me, at times you represented the audience. Using Undeniably Truthful Statements and forced mind reads.

I know you're wondering if it's really that easy.

Simplicity of the skills and techniques lies in the application and level of rapport with your listeners. This is not hard to do by any stretch of the imagination. It takes a little practice and concentrated effort and that's about it.

Is it easy? I don't know, that depends on you I guess. I developed this method of selling years ago and it has served me and my clients well over the years. It is non-evasive, non-intrusive, not abrasive in its approach and eliminates buyer's remorse with every prospect.

No harsh closing techniques, no psychological traps to back the prospect into a verbal corner. Which is of paramount importance in network marketing, if you have to sell your prospect on the idea once, you will have to do it again and again. However if they join for their reasons, and they uncover their compelling reason why in the process, you don't have to sell them on the idea or concept again.

The first sale that must be made is "you" being sold on the service or product. Once the prospect sells themselves with your guidance, you never have to sell them again.

UTS… as you sit there reading the words on this page, thinking to yourself, "can it really be that simple?"

You already know the answer.

How About the Free Secret?

Maybe you would not pay a million dollars for the secret, how about if I were to give it to you for **FREE**? Would you take it then?

What do you think would happen if you gave out free $100.00 bills? Most likely on the street of the average city no one will take it, or at least very few people would take it.

You have a better chance of getting robbed than you would of just giving money away for nothing.

The information about undeniably truthful statements is important for you to understand and be able to use for your future success. It is yours here for free; you can also find it in Dr. Donald Moine's book, Unlimited Selling Power, and Dr. Kevin Hogan's book Psychology of Persuasion and Dr. Robert Cialdini's book the Psychology of Persuasion it's not as obvious, you have to look for it.

You can do a search online and see if you can find information about it there.

I am sure you will find there is not much information about UTS online.

So would this be classified as a "**SECRET**?" *[The particular knowledge and skills needed to do something very well - Kept hidden from knowledge or view; concealed. - Something kept hidden from others or known only to oneself or to a few.]* I'd say that's a bona fide secret.

I am sure you would agree a secret would be worth knowing,

especially if it could unlock the door to riches of unknown wealth? Like the secret to a buried treasure. The contents of the treasure chest itself might be worthless; however the secret to its whereabouts could be worth untold millions.

This secret is actually worth millions, but on the surface it may look worthless, however to the few who understand it's true worth, the secret has unlocked wealth of countless millions. Who knows the real value of UTS?

Kevin Hogan	Joe Vitale
Jay Abraham	Donald Moine
John Grinder	Robert G. Allen
Tony Robbins	Richard Bandler

I am sure there might be a few other people that might know, however I do not know of them.

UTS, is definitely a secret in the real sense of the word.

However it is not going to divulge any national secrets should you learn a little about it and use it to create for yourself and your family the wealth you deserve.

What about mismatchers?...

Mismatchers are a unique group of people, not a bad group of people, just a unique group of people.

Within the mismatcher group there is what is known as the "Polarity Mismatcher." These kinds of people if you are not prepared can try your patience to their limits. These are the types of people no matter what you say, undeniable or not, they will ALWAYS find the difference, or the exception and point it out, and when you agree with them on their point they will proceed to disagree with their own statement.

To find out if you are a mismatcher or not take this little harmless test.

Below you will find pictures of 4 U.S. quarters, simply explain their relationship to each other.

The average person will usually answer something like:

They are all quarters   all worth .25   they are in a line

They are shiny   three are heads up   evenly spaced apart

they appear to be the same year   The heads and tails are odd number.... and so on.

The mismatcher on the other hand is quite an obvious difference in their answers.

One is tails, they are not all facing the same direction, they are not evenly spaced apart, there is an odd number of heads, They all seem to be worth .25, but have to check on the series to make sure one or more are not worth more to a collector.

I think you get the idea.

When dealing with mismatchers it is important to make sure you are using UTS as much as possible to avoid a confrontation.

Is it good to be a mismatcher? YES, if you are an attorney, architect, engineer, scientist, or physicist, and a few other professions, nonetheless, it's not a good idea not to bring your mismatching habits home with you.

When dealing with a mismatcher in your network marketing business it could prove frustrating. Mismatchers will typically be the most frustrating of representatives, they will not follow your advice, they will not follow the crowd, the will question everything, and eventually they will leave to find an organization that better suits them.

Keep in mind this is not "set in stone," it is however a generality. Not every mismatcher will do that, however it does happen enough, making it a good idea to identify this situation early in your organization and utilize your time accordingly.

Now I know I am going to get tons of emails telling me, "I'm a mismatcher and I have been with my network marketing company for seven years and I resent you saying I will hop from one to the next." or something along those lines. My answer to that is, "you are the exception, and I will reiterate, this is a generality, and not a rule that is set in stone."

Your Appearance

UTS can also be assessed by your appearance, if you come across someone who claims to be successful, and they are not dressed well, as in, ripped, tattered, torn, and worn out clothes, and generally not very well kept; wearing clothing that is not consistent with someone who is successful, this could be viewed as incongruent, giving off a message to the listener that something is not right and up go the walls of resistance.

This does not mean that you need to dress like a millionaire, and wear $5,000.00 suits, and $18,000.00 dresses, or wear gold and jewelry and drive a big fancy car and live in a mansion.

It does mean that you should take care of the way you look and the clothes you wear, making sure you do not look tattered and torn when you should look crisp and clean.

If you cannot afford to buy the nicer clothes, then at least you can afford to take care of the clothes you have, making sure to leave a lasting positive impression with the people you meet.

I rarely wear a suit these days, and when I do wear a suit it is for a special occasion, even when I do my events I am in jeans or something relaxed and casual. Nonetheless, the look is crisp and clean, up to date, and appropriate, leaving a lasting impression with the people I meet.

When you get dressed be thinking in the back of your mind, "who will I see today, and who will see me?"

How you dress is not as important to you, as it is to the people you will meet.

Recently I was with a friend of mine who was visiting from Southeast Asia, we were in Houston at the time and she wanted to go shopping. So we went to a very exclusive part of Houston, the shops all cater to the upper income crowds and nonetheless she was impressed. She asked me how can she tell who is really wealthy and who is faking it.

I took her into an exclusive body lotions shop and let her look around, there were three types of people in the store. The socially conscious types who have some money and want chemical free soaps and lotions, the lookie-loos, and the very wealthy.

She could see the difference immediately, even if they were in jeans, flip-flops and a t-shirt, their wealth was obvious, from the way they carried themselves to the labels they wore. The thing that stuck out with her the most is how easily she could spot this difference.

She would strike up conversations with them and learn more about them, and the wealthier clientele were the ones easiest to talk to.

One even invited her to dinner and as it turned out the woman that invited my friend to dinner was a top income earner in a multi-level company

Your clothes and the way you carry yourself, your attitude, your demeanor, can say a lot about who you are, make sure it is a congruent message about you.

For an individual to move with confidence in the world, a person must have
a wardrobe that suits him/her and his/her style of living. It is a task that required nuanced understanding of both fashion and oneself, (two areas of inquiry; many are prone to ignore), as well as a firm, grasp of the state of one's exchequer. Building a wardrobe is a lifetime pursuit, a journey rather than a destination.

What message is your wardrobe sending to your prospects and business associates? Is it congruent with whom you are and where you are headed? Is it congruent with the message you are delivering to those you come in contact with on a daily basis?

Imagine for a moment, you go to a professional football game, and the teams are running out onto the field. The opposition to your favorite team takes the field first. The team runs out on to the field, dressed in their uniforms, their pads, looking mean, tough as hell, and ready for battle. Then your team takes the field running out on to the field wearing baseball uniforms. Brand new, crisp sharp looking uniforms. Specially designed ball caps and the whole works. What team do you think will win? I am betting the team that showed up to play football will be the winner today. Call me silly or old-fashioned but that is my guess.

Think about that when you get dressed tomorrow, what game are you dressed for? Are you dressed for the right game? Are you playing in the right league? What do your fans think when they see you out on the playing field of your life, do they think you are dressed for the right game?

Tapestry of Words...

Using your words, to create phrases, stories, and metaphors, weaving them into artful masterpieces that can induce the emotions and mental pictures that best aligns with your listener.

The combination of words and science…"*Recent trends in neuroscience and information theory view the brain, mind, and behavior as networked information-sharing systems.*

The scientific basis for Neuro-Behavioral Programs is the phenomenon called information transduction. In this well-researched phenomenon, information from words and images (psyche) is translated into information that can be received and processed within these networked subsystems in the body (soma). Simply put, words or pictures in the mind or imagination can trigger physical changes in the body."

The program mentioned above is for pain management; just imagine if you were to use my Neuro-Behavioral Wealth conditioning Program, for wealth management, and wealth creation. How much of your behavior could you direct and control towards the attainment of your goals, if you had a system designed to maximize the effects the words you use on your physical world and the attainment of your goals?

Make no mistakes about it the effect your words can have on your listener is real.

The effect your words have on you is just as real!

Sample Script:

Imagine as I begin to program the computer I call my mind, now. The new program is a program designed to delete negative thoughts and negative suggestions, and to completely eliminate any negative influence they may have on me at any level in my mind. All thoughts and suggestions that
might be detrimental to my health, wealth, and happiness are deleted and their effects are not only neutralized, the effects are turned into a super powerful positive mental energy juice. My mind is tuned into success frequencies that release avalanches of abundance and prosperity upon me. I am now becoming more and more receptive to the conditions and circumstances that are beneficial to my health, wealth and happiness.

Seeing me in my mind's eye as a multi-millionaire, thinking like a millionaire, walking, talking, believing, feeling and acting like the millionaire I am deep within. My mind allowing the inner millionaire in me to emerge and live a life of fulfillment and abundance.

Like a WIFI connection to the Internet, my mind picks up the frequency of millionaire minds, conditioning my mind to think of abundance, prosperity, and opportunity.

I can visualize and imagine in vivid color as I reprogram the computer I call my mind, now. The program of wealth and abundance, weeding out the weeds and negativity and replacing them with a garden filled with the seeds of prosperity and abundance, blossoming into the fulfilled dreams of my mind and heart.

4 Powers of the Universe

There are said to be 4 major powers of the Universe, those are:

Money   **Beauty**   **Force**   **Persuasion**

Of these 4 powers which do you think are the most powerful?

It might not be what you think so pick carefully.

Money is not it; force, beauty and persuasion can take the money. It is not force, money beauty and persuasion can utilize force and strip it of its power.

Beauty is the answer, money force and persuasion cannot take beauty from the one who has it. They can attempt to hold it captive but they can never take it away and have it for themselves.

The second most powerful is persuasion. With the right persuasion you can literally control vast fortunes and governments. Combine beauty and persuasion and you can control the universe, the universe will bend to your will.

Which Brings This Little Book to an End....

But that does not have to be the end of the story...

You can go on with this information and create some great things in your life, should you decide to do so.

The SECRETS held within the pages of this little book are real secrets by definition, and you like so many others before you can go out armed with this little gem in your arsenal of success practices
and achieve some amazing things.

What will you do with this information? Will you use it and add it to your tool box of success tools, or will you walk right past?

The problem with giving away a secret like this, is a lot like planting seeds blindly, one never really knows if the seed is on fertile ground or not. The only way to tell is to wait and watch and see if the seed begins to sprout, and grow. Even if the seed does sprout and grows will it succumb to the elements? The only defense the little plant has is to have deep and wide roots, to keep it solidly planted when the winds of trial begin to blow.

What will you do with this information?

Pop Quiz Time

1. What should you do if you like this book?

    A. Delete it   B. Save it   C. Share it   D. Unsure, need to re-read it

2. What are the 2 things you cannot do with this book? _____ & _____

3. This book does not constitute P_____ or T_____ advice in any way shape or form.

4. Who is this book for? _____

5. None of the concepts discussed in this book will work if you:

   A. Mix them with milk and cookies   B. Serve them over French Toast
   C. Never try them   D. All of the above

6. What is this book about? _____
    Saying what you _____, _____ what you say, and saying it with _____

   A. Mean   B. Meaning   C. Cooking   D. Swimming   E. Taste
   F. Communication   G. Curiosity   H. Sleeping   I. Meaning   J. Reading

7. What is the leading cause of miscommunication?

   A_____ C_____.

8. How do you make seven even?

   A. Take a way one   B. Take a way S   C. Add one   D. You can't

9. What is the title of this book? _____ _____

   _____

10. A butcher is 6'7" tall, wears size 18 shoes, and has a 50" waist. What does the butcher weigh?

    A. 350 lbs   B. 400 lbs   C. Not enough facts   D. Meat

11. What would it be like if all your communication was with meaning and congruent?

12. Who is it that said if you want to act powerfully you need to master "speech acts"

    A. Leonardo Da Vinci   B. Fernando Flores
    C. Albert Einstein   D. Captain Crunch

Oops my bad, looks like I was wrong, question 13 seems to have sprouted legs and walked right off the page, leaving footprints behind.

13   13   13   13
  13   13

14. Beginning of eternity
The end of space
The beginning of every end
The end of every place
What am I?

A. Time   B. Thought   C. Butter Fly Affect   D. Letter "E"

15. U.T.S means?

A. Universally Transmitted Slime

B. Unidentifiable Tactile Statehood

C. Unidentified Silly Transmutations

C 1/2 Undeniably Truthful Statements

D. Unidentified Tossed Saucers

16. Who is buried in Grants tomb?
A. Outlaw Josey Wales   B. General Custer   C. Grant   D. Washington

17. Describe a mismatcher and name 2 people who fit this description.
_____
_____
_____

18. When a sales person is talking to me in a store what do I consider a big plus?

   A. Not standing on my foot   B. Taking a breath mint
   C. Not drinking on the job   D. All of the above

19. What book did Donald Moine write?

   A. The Bible   B. Unlimited Selling Power   C. Charlottes Tree House

20. What interests you most about Network Marketing?
   _____
   _____
   _____

21. What is the very closely guarded secret?
   _____
   _____
   _____

Notes

22. What does **U.U.T.S** mean?

_____
_____
_____

23. Why do you spill the milk right after you are reminded not to?

    A. You fell asleep   B. Your brain went for a walk and left your nose in charge
    C. You forgot the question   D. Forced Mind Read

24. What playing card from the deck was the last card?

_____

25. What is the Million Dollar Secret?

_____
_____
_____

26. What is the relationship of the quarters to each other?

_____
_____
_____

27. Who is going to see you today, or who did see you today?

_____
_____
_____

What do you think their impression of you and your attire was?

_____
_____

28. What is the name of the book from where this quote came from? "*In order to move with confidence in the world, a man must have a wardrobe that suits him and his style of living. It is a task that required nuanced understanding of both fashion and oneself, (two areas of inquiry many men are prone to ignore), as well as a firm, grasp of the state of one's exchequer. Building a wardrobe is a lifetime pursuit, a journey rather than a destination.*"

   A. As a Man Thinketh
   B. The Bible
   C. Science of Moon Travel
   D. Men's Wardrobe

29. Recent trends in neuroscience and _____ view the brain, mind and behavior as networked information sharing systems.

30. What is the name of the technology I designed for wealth management and wealth creation?

_____

31. Your mind is like a WIFI connection picking up the frequency of _____ conditioning your mind for think of _____, _____, _____ .

32. Number 1 power in the universe is _____
    explain how that impacts your life
    _____
    _____
    _____

33. What message does the **_BOLD Italicized Underlined Letters_** found throughout this book spell out?
    *Example: (**_K_**)*
    _____
    _____

    (write the letters in order found - there are 15 words, 1 punctuation, total 55 letters)

    _____
    _____
    _____
    (write the message here)

34. How many people will you pass this book on to? Name at least 4.

    _____
    _____
    _____
    _____

More to Come....

I realize the best way to get my ideas, theories and concepts to spread to as many people as possible was to write books. Books that inspire, motivate and educate, books that take the reader one step beyond where they were when they began reading. I believe everything happens for a reason and a purpose and it serves our higher self. There is a reason you have this book in your possession, it is not an accident that you are reading this now.

> **Then indecision brings its own delays,**
> **and days are lost lamenting over lost days.**
> **Are you in earnest? Seize this very minute;**
> **What you can do, or dream you can do, begin it;**
> **Boldness has genius, power and magic in it.**
>   "Goethe"

I thank you for reading and I look forward to sharing some time together again in the future. If you have any questions, Suggestions, or requests please contact me at
LISA@DRLISACOACHING.COM

If you would like to be notified of future books please send an e-mail to LISA@DRLISACOACHING.COM
also you can request my latest books on AMAZON and
www.drlisacoaching.com